MW01047330

Table of Contents

BLUES & OTHER HUES

Ryan Fraley
(ASCAP)

JAVA

Ryan Fraley
(ASCAP)

COLD CANYON

Ryan Fraley
(ASCAP)

Cold Canyon

RHYTHM BEE

Ryan Fraley
(ASCAP)

Guitar / Vibes

SLOW BURN

Ryan Fraley
(ASCAP)

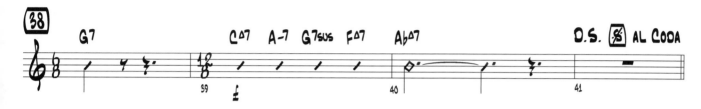

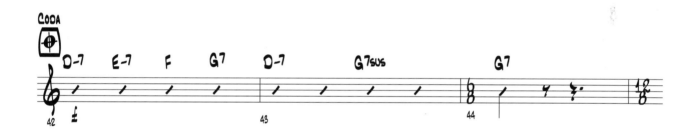

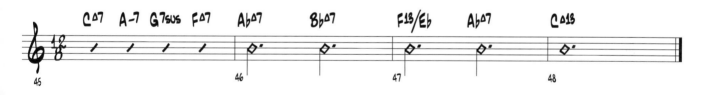

Guitar / Vibes

PROG PACIFIC

Ryan Fraley
(ASCAP)

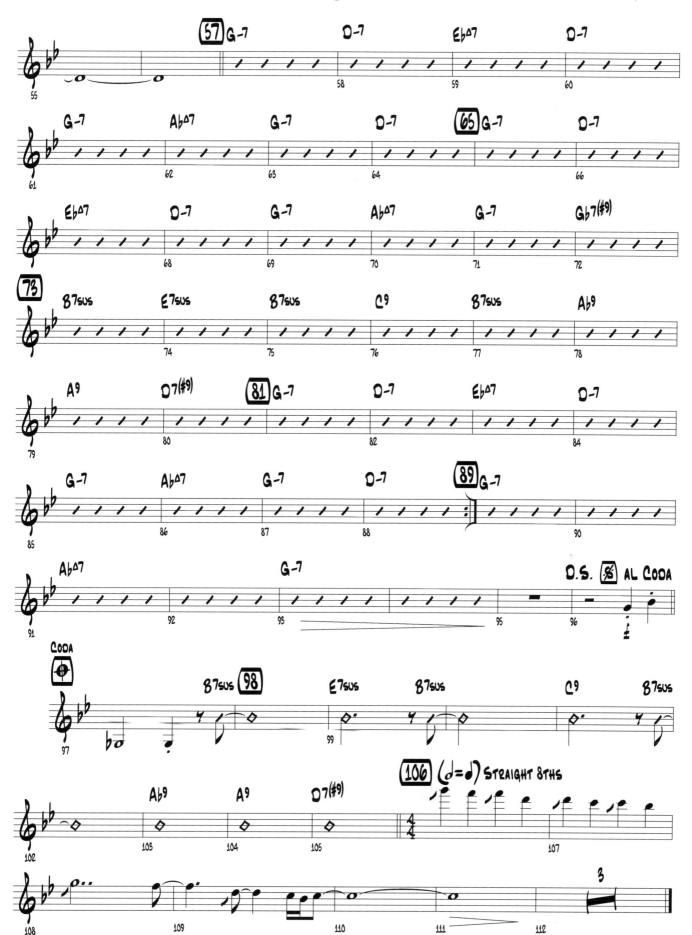

Prog Pacific

SOLO TRANSCRIPTION

as played by Isaac Helbling (Guitar)

SOLO TRANSCRIPTION

as played by Sylvain Carton (Alto Sax)

Java

SOLO TRANSCRIPTION

as played by Ryan Fraley (Trombone)

Rhythm Bee

SOLO TRANSCRIPTION

as played by Alex Noppe (Trumpet)

½ VALVE (TPT.)

LAY BACK

Slow Burn

SOLO TRANSCRIPTION

as played by Sylvain Carton (Alto Sax)

Slow Burn

Prog Pacific

SOLO TRANSCRIPTION

as played by Alex Noppe (Trumpet)

(GUITAR CHORDS)

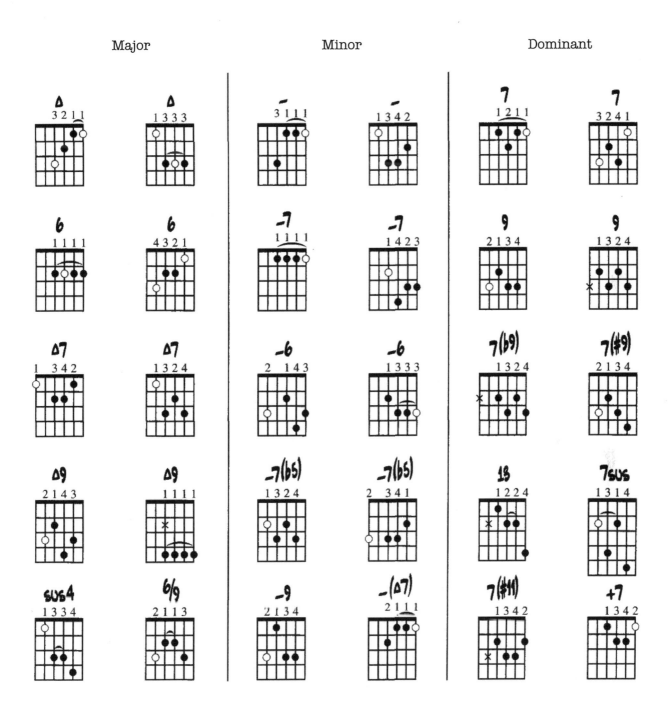

o = root
x = root (don't play)

(PLAY-ALONG TRACKS)

Recordings and play-along tracks for all six tunes can be found here:

www.ryanfraley.com

∿ For each tune, there are 8 versions:

Full mix

Rhythm Section Only

Play-Along as Part 1

Play-Along as Part 2

Play-Along as Part 3

Play-Along as Piano / Guitar

Play-Along as Bass

Play-Along as Drums

Use this QR Code to access a player loaded with all 48 Audio Tracks:
You may download them and save locally if you wish.

Made in the USA
Middletown, DE
11 May 2024

54215452R00015